Citizenship

Being Honest

Cassie Mayer

Heinemann Library
Chicago, Illinois

Customer Service 888-454-2279
Visit our website at www.heinemannraintree.com

Designed by Joanna Hinton-Malivoire
Illustrated by Mark Beech
Printed and bound in China by South China Printing Co. Ltd.

11 10 09 08 07
10 9 8 7 6 5 4 3 2 1

The Library of Congress has cataloged the first edition of this book as follows:
Mayer, Cassie.
 Being honest / Cassie Mayer.
    p. cm. -- (Citizenship)
 Includes bibliographical references and index.
 ISBN 978-1-4034-9484-9 (hc) -- ISBN 978-1-4034-9492-4 (pb) 1. Honesty--Juvenile literature. I. Title.
 BJ1533.H7M39 2007
 179'.9--dc22
                              2006039376

Contents

Being honest means telling
the truth.

Being honest means people can
trust you.

When you return something that
is not yours ...

you are being honest.

When you show someone you
made a mess ...

you are being honest.

When you tell someone you made
a mistake ...

you are being honest.

When you say, "I had my share" ...

you are being honest.

When you say, "I had my turn" ...

you are being honest.

When you tell someone how
you feel …

you are being honest.

When you admit that you
were wrong ...

you are being honest.

Being honest is important.

How can you be honest?

Activity

How is this child being honest?

Picture Glossary

 **admit** tell something that you may be afraid to tell

 **honest** always telling the truth

 **trust** to believe in someone

Index

Note to Parents and Teachers
Each book in this series shows examples of behavior that demonstrate good citizenship. Take time to discuss each illustration and ask children to identify the honest behavior shown. Use the question on page 21 to ask students how they can be honest in their own lives.

The text has been chosen with the advice of a literacy expert to enable beginning readers success while reading independently or with moderate support. You can support children's nonfiction literacy skills by helping them use the table of contents, picture glossary, and index.